AF395060

dot

an
artist's
guide

eastwinterbooks.com/dot

By Luxandbolts
Edited by Murasak.E
Curated by OutofTokyo

First edition, for version 0.6, published by East Winter® Books
an imprint of Thought and Company Ltd,
33 London N7 0HU
www.eastwinter.com

Book design and production by East Winter® Books.
Set in IBM Plex.

ISBN: 978-0-9935046-4-8

Contents

Preamble

'dot' is a homemade web-app [0] drawing environment specifically designed for creating abstracted connect-the-dot drawings. The notion of choosing the dot-to-dot as a drawing method came through a wish to invite others to connect (or ignore) the dots, to participate in creating a modified but continuously abstract work.

This exercise and amateur experiment in code, given the author's limited skill, has no interest in competing with professional level applications, instead retains its origins in a curiosity for the range of abstracted interactive drawing types of crosswords, colouring drawings, Sudoku's, and spot the difference drawings, leading to the notion of the Dot-to-dot as abstract composition, with interactive potential.

Of what is produced, how much of a work is touched by the 'way' of the drawing tool used, its nature (the way it wants to be used given its required process, and the other tools with which it may interact), and the way of its situating environment—affecting a state of mind (or way) in which others experience the work? As we as designers so rarely get a chance to build a drawing application from scratch, this was an opportunity for personal reflection that played into meditations on our relationship with our adopted digital tools, how we design within and through given software frameworks—digital environments developed [for good reason] by specialists but rarely creative end users. In which subtle ways do we adapt to our tools, in which subtle ways might these internal technical tendencies affect a work? How do we judge the limits of where these interactions are compromised, or successful?

The following works are playful explorations of the tool, developed by various invited artists. The works of the second half, following the guide itself, are by luxandbolts and indulge in the abstracted dot-to-dot.

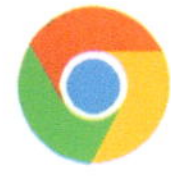
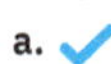
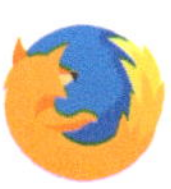

a. ✔ b. ✔ c. ✘

0a. Dot was written on Chrome (mac) Laptop and so this is the preferred optimum working environment.
Touch-screen support is very limited as Dot requires Mouse functions: hover, precision, left+right buttons, and the mouse wheel.

0b. Appears to be happy on Firefox.
Based on lackadaisical tests.

0c. Safari does not play well with dot!
Due to the browser itself currently not properly displaying Brush (BRSH) tool attributes. To print from Safari; use File > 'Export as PDF...' from the main application menu.

0+. Other Browsers: Have a go and see what happens?

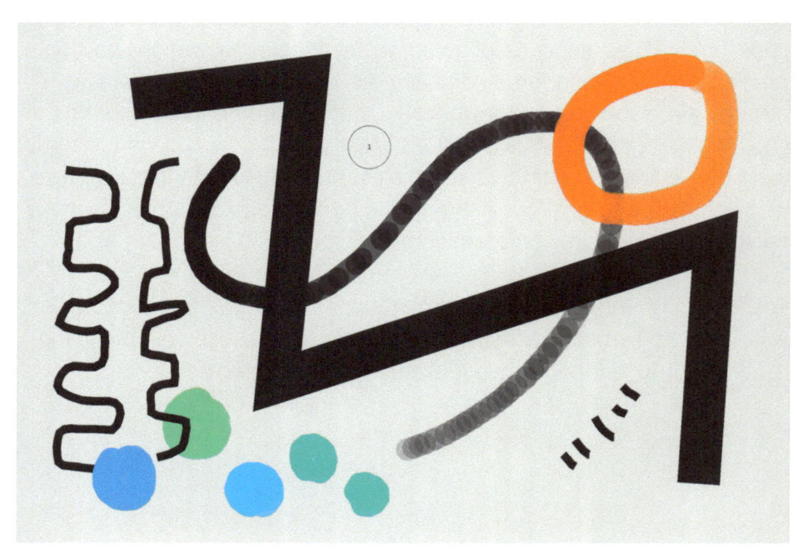

Untitled. YM.

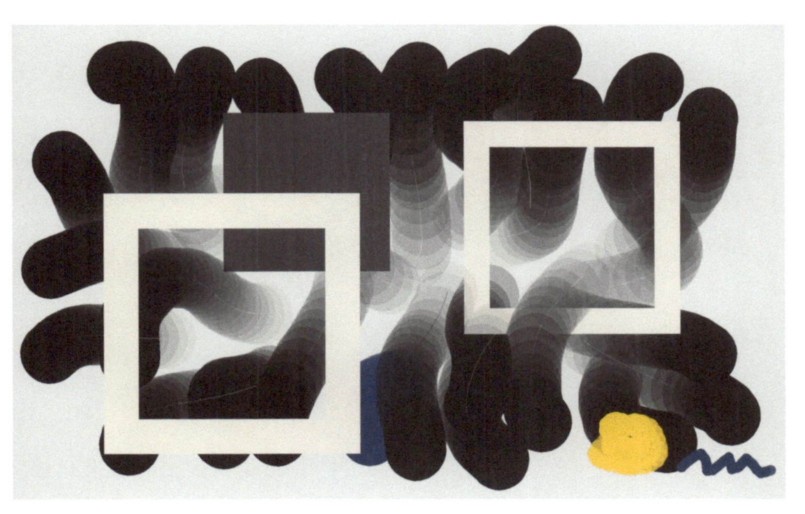

Untitled. YM.

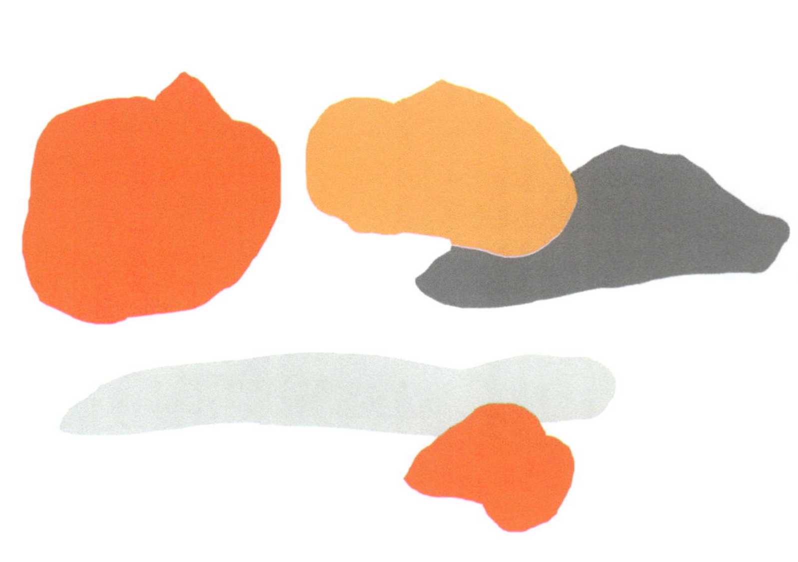

Untitled. Seafoampolkadots.

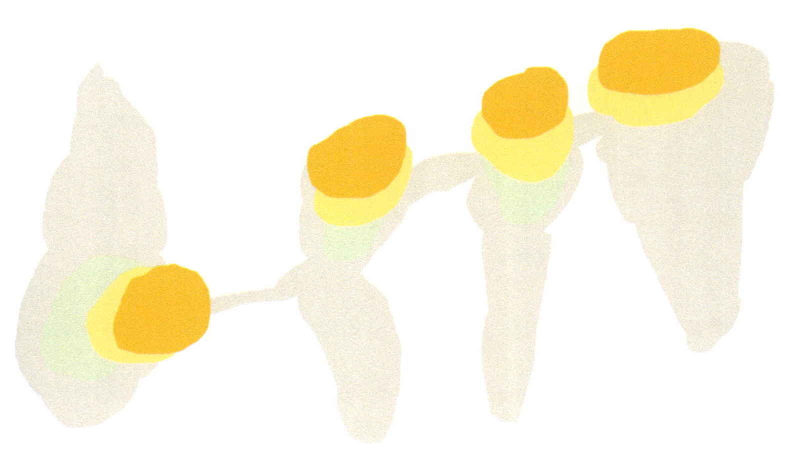

Untitled. Seafoampolkadots.

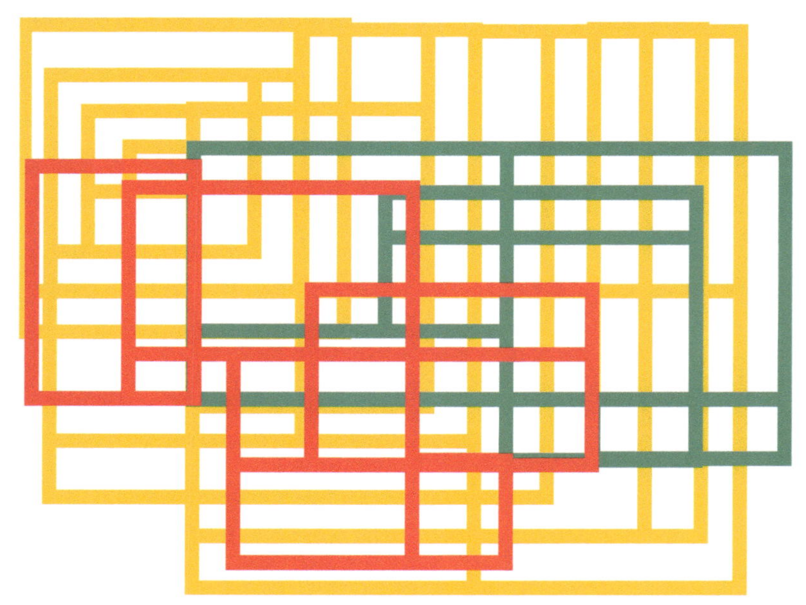

Untitled. Outlier.

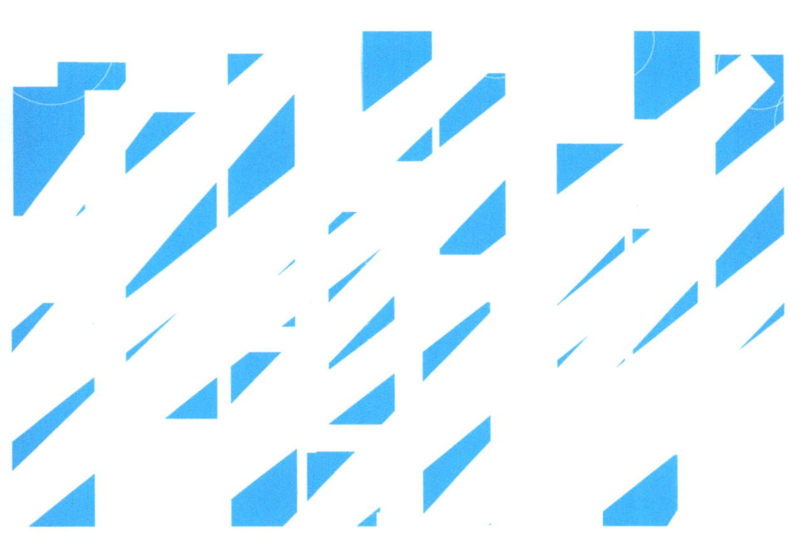

Untitled. Outlier.

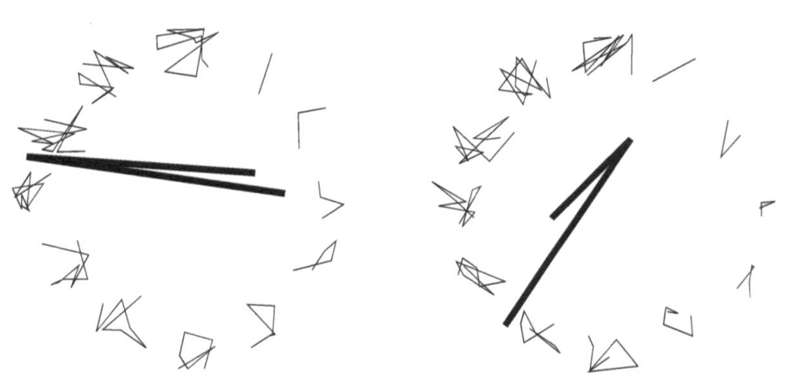

with love for FGT. Outlier

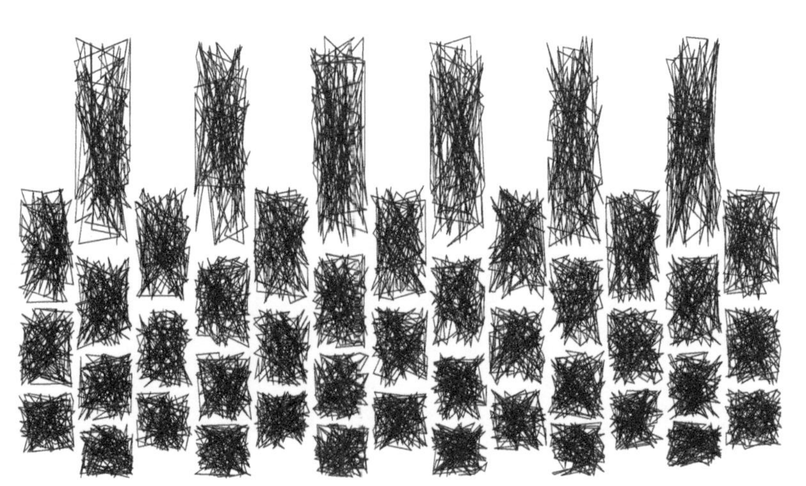

logarithmic. Outlier

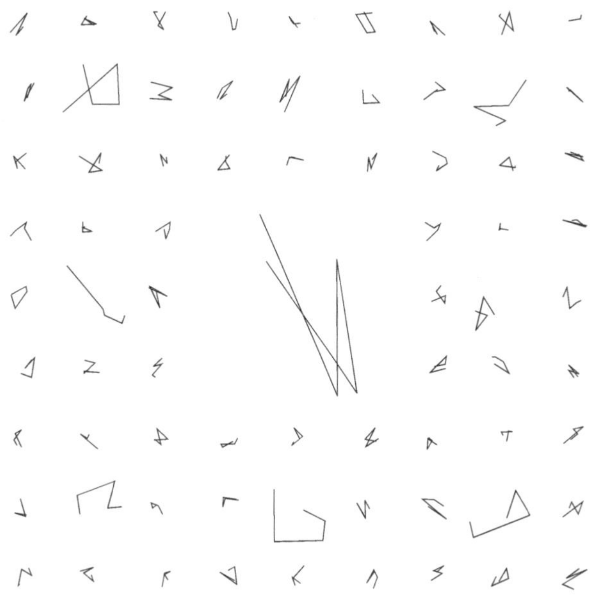

Carpet 5. Outlier

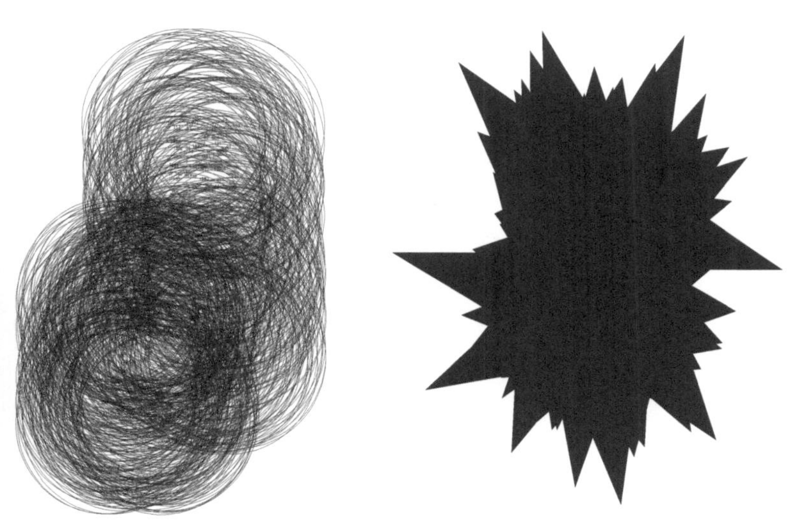

Twins. Outlier

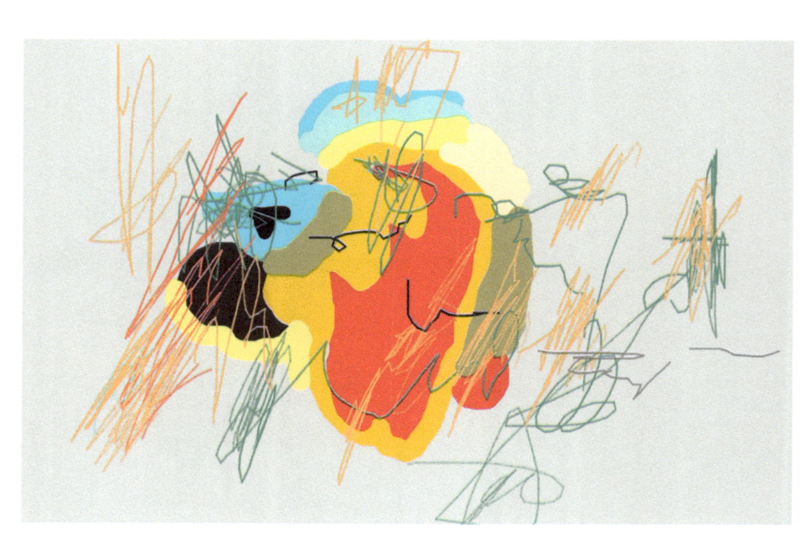

Untitled (Thought no.1). Nari

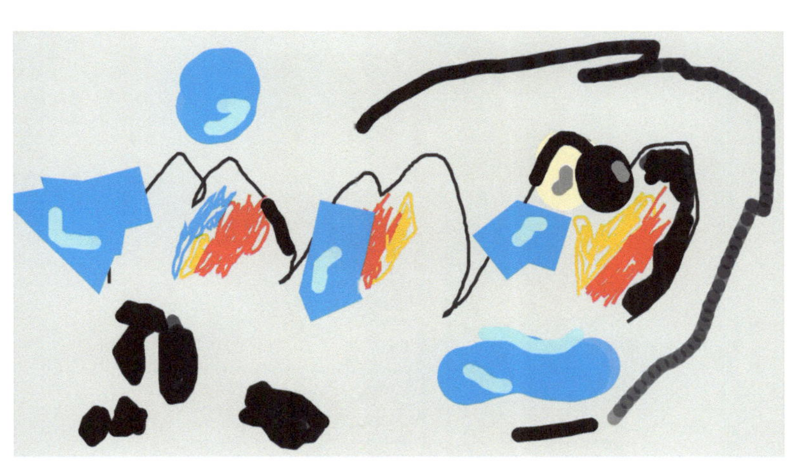

Untitled (Thought no.2). Nari

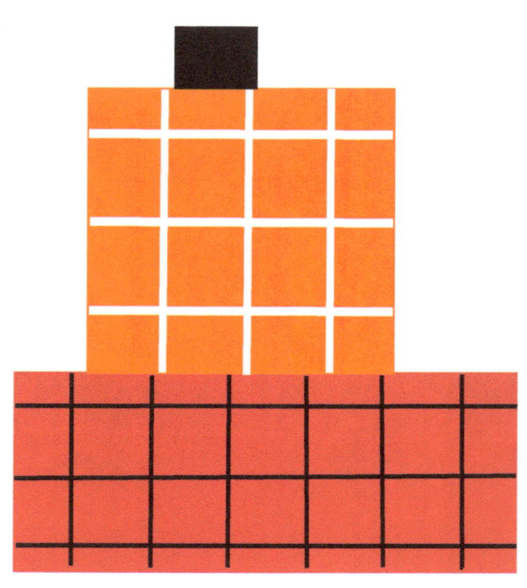

No title (I), AK

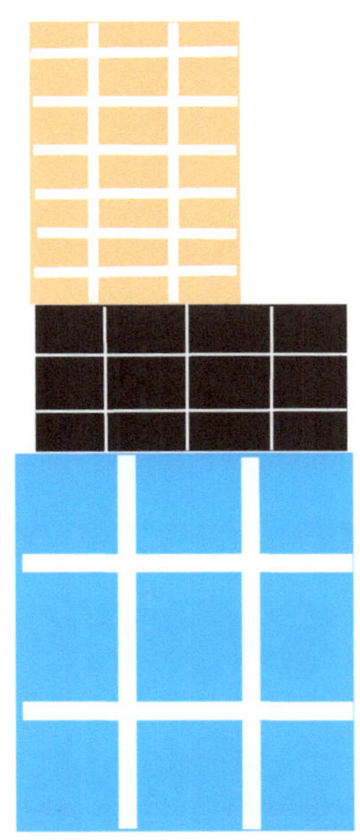

No title (II), AK

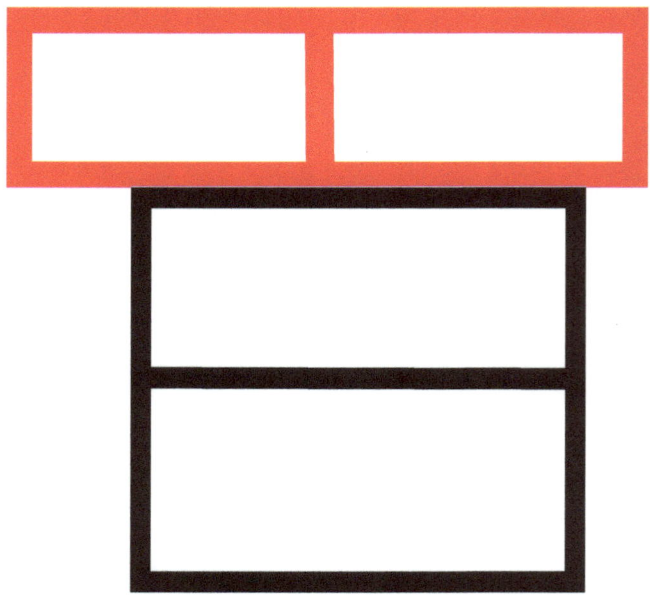

Structure (a), AK

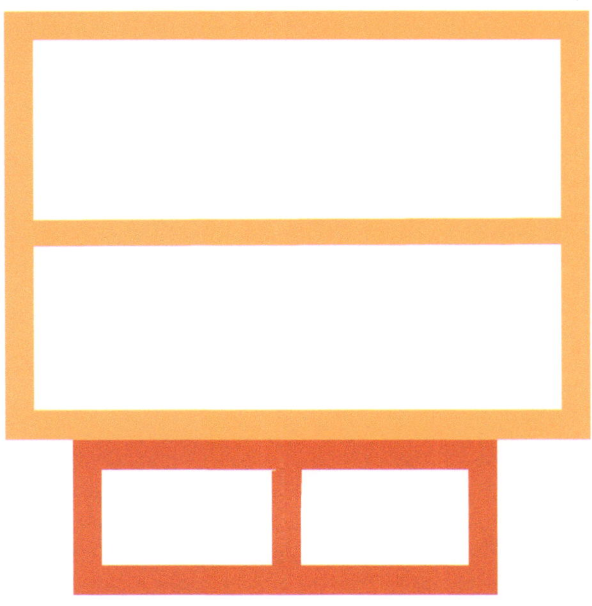

Structure (b), AK

dot · 'Made to make dot-to-dots'

Hello, hi and welcome to Dot.

Sometimes passing interests, available facilities, and situations combine fortuitously. In this case; the passing interest was in particular modes of abstract expression, or simply a broad spread of visual compositions typified by the likes of Joan Mitchell and Cy Twombly through Pierre Soulages to Julie Mehretu, Ronan Bouroullec, Helen O'Leary, Sara Barker, Marc Nagtzaam, and Kees Goudzwaard. The facility was an online development platform, and the situation framed the time and space unfortunately afforded by the first lock-down of 2020. The former developed through the idea of creating (instead of a collection of works) a private–public facility, a digital studio space, as a web-based fully functioning app accessible to many—itself built through a web-based app facility accessible to many. The latter part; time, coincided with being an architect (of buildings), with amateur skills in front-end web development. However, with time, its features expanded. To a place where some of its abilities needed further description to enable you, the artist, to get the most out of this exercise.

How to access Dot

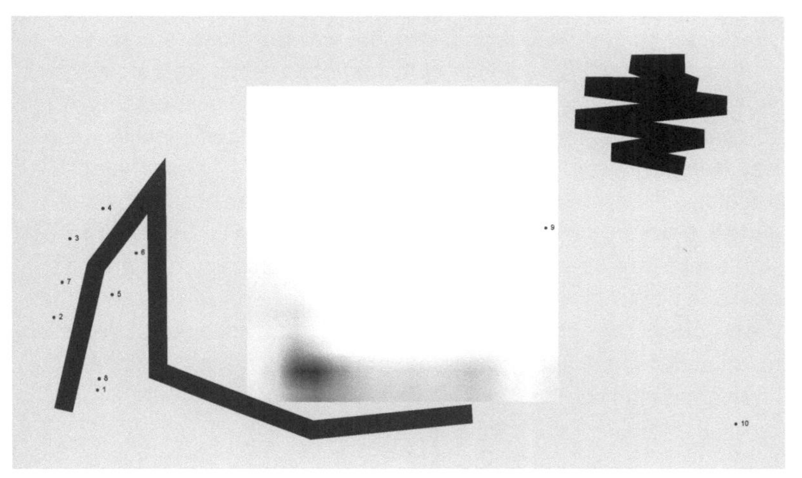

The first drawing output. luxandbolts.

Interests

The name 'dot' sprung from the earlier interest, the idea of the Dot-to-dot drawing [a.k.a join-the-dot, or connect-the-dots] as a base mode of abstraction (notionally complete), but with an added interactive dimension; engaging audience participation to complete it a second time. Typically, a Dot-to-dot composition moves from something abstract to something figurative, as most outcomes become in some way recognisable you would be forgiven for wanting to continue this tradition. However, to recall the original inspirations of composition and abstraction, the passing interest here began in creating dot-to-dot works that start as abstract and transition...to abstract. Arguably, if a resulting work has no referential intentions, then does it matter if the viewer obeys the numeric flow, or even the dots themselves? What are the qualities of the line or point that makes any one composition more interesting than another?

In practice, for many professional creatives working today, a large portion of the work we do is conducted through some form of software environment; beneath the roof of Adobe, or Autodesk, or Bentley and so on, each with its own complex of behavioural rules. Similar could perhaps be said of painters' studios; the realisation of a work, interpreted from an inner world, within the framework of an existing architectural space, whether digital or physical. Yet it might be more common that artists have a hand in the creation of their spaces or, at the very least, the possibility. With examples ranging from DIY garden shed studio's, to tailorec commissioned industrial scale new-builds, artist designers tend to have more scope for shaping their physical environments than we do as designers or artists in affecting the architecture of the software environments we so often practice through. As such; dot is an experiment, from this brief meditation, by an architect, in creating a drawing application. If Adobe is a village, Autocad a building, then (Dot) is a small coffee-table, or maybe a hutch for a pet hamster; where this author is the hamster.

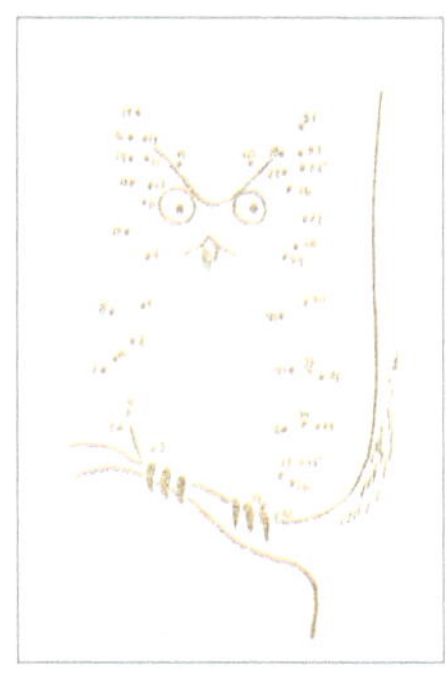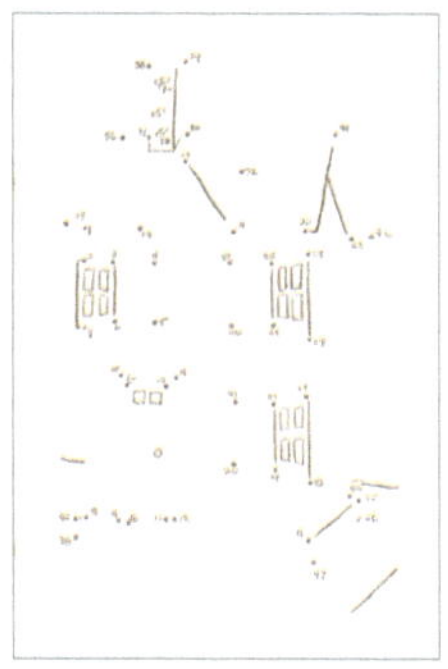

Dot Shapes Activity Book. Herther Depper, 1966

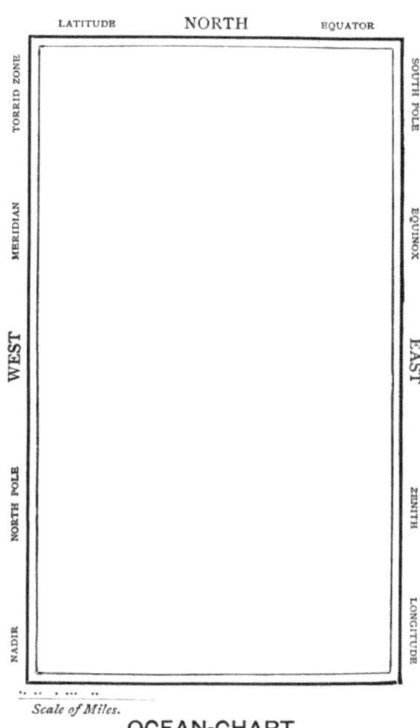

Above. The fourth of Henry Holiday's original ilustrations to "The Hunting of the Snark: An Agony in Eight Fits" by Lewis Carroll. 1931. An indirect inspiration for Dot's interface layout. 'From Fit the Second: The Bellman's Speech. This shows the Bellman's map, which, being blank, is equally useful everywhere, unlike normal maps'

The Hunting of the Snark: The Ocean Chart

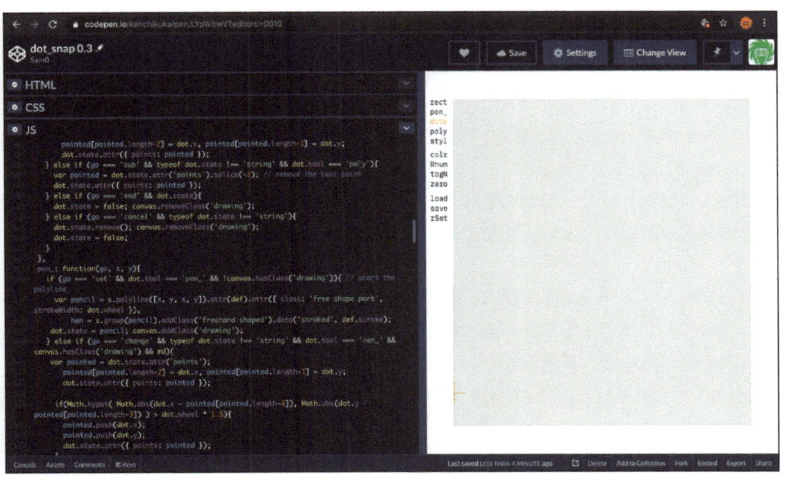

Dot: in progress

Facility

And would it be interesting if more designers would (or could) make or even just assemble software if they chose—given the possibility? The same way an artist might curate, compose, and customise her studio space—perhaps with a homemade table, or a bespoke easel swapped in from another maker? And so from the interests, to the facility itself, we have dot: designed as a Web-app with no need to install or update, and largely platform agnostic—though it wants a mouse! [1] dot was made entirely with Codepen.io, another web based coding workbench, but only tested on the Chrome browser for now [2].

Dot uses more of your mouse than most web pages. To get started it is important to know the **left-mouse-button** *DRAWS* stuff, the **right-mouse-button** *SELECTS* stuff to change, and the **mouse-wheel** [3] *SIZES* stuff once selected. Selection works by toggling (select / deselect), from where you can scale, drag, rotate, increase line thickness, change colours (shift-key short-cut), or delete, plus bottom left corner (**sub-menu**) screen options as they appear depending on which tool is active. **Tools appear when the mouse leaves the canvas (or tap on the space-bar).**

1. **Dot interacts very differently with touch-screens, here a first contact positions the cursor. A second additional 'tap' anywhere to the left reflects a 'left-mouse-button' mouse-click. A tap anywhere to the right of the cursor reflects a 'right-mouse-button' click.** You might find this takes some practice, but hopefully you'll see it allows for precision input and greater functionality on a touch-screen.

2. **The remainder of this booklet will describe the app on the basis of this configuration of hardware/software.**

3. **If using a laptop trackpad without a mouse, the two finger scroll technique is often interpreted as a wheel substitute.**

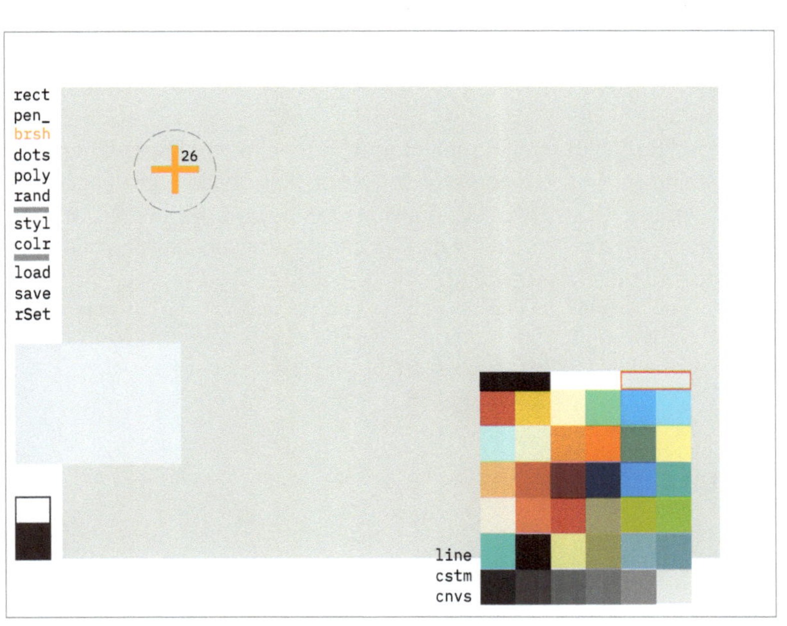

Dot's basic layout: Main menu, Style transfer area, and Colour palette

This should be enough to get started. You, as artist, are encouraged to play and explore all menu options framing the canvas drawing area.

Note that the STYL (machine-learning style transfer implementation of Magentaimage.js [4] and incorporating Tensor-flow [5]) has a very specific method of use. Other than this, drawings can be saved or loaded, and image (and native '.dots') drawing files can be dragged in from your desktop into the drawing area [6].

Situation

Beyond, the remainder of this text aims to describe a few of the less obvious tricks and techniques available.

4. Interpreted from https://magenta.
    github.io/magenta-js/image/ based on
    a machine–learning research paper by:

    Ghiasi, G., Lee, H., Kudlur, M., Dumoulin,
    V. and Shlens, J. (2017) *Exploring
    the structure of a real-time, arbitrary
    neural artistic stylization network*,
    arXiv:1705.06830 [cs]. Available at:
    http://arxiv.org/abs/1705.06830

5. TensorFlow is an open-source
    software library developed by Google.
    It is a symbolic math library, and is used
    here to support Magenta.js.

6. No drawings or images are returned
    to a server. This site is designed to
    be client based, and thus loading and
    saving of drawings happens locally
    independently of eastwinter.com

DO   **Left-mouse-button**: Most drawing tools are brought into effect on a tap-by-tap basis, except the **_pen** and **brsh** (Brush) tools which prefer movement whilst pressing this button.

RESIZE   **Mouse-wheel**: This sets the line width for the next drawing element. Alternatively, if you use the **rndm** tool, the wheel number sets the number or corners before use. The wheel also works simultaneously with the **brsh** tool.

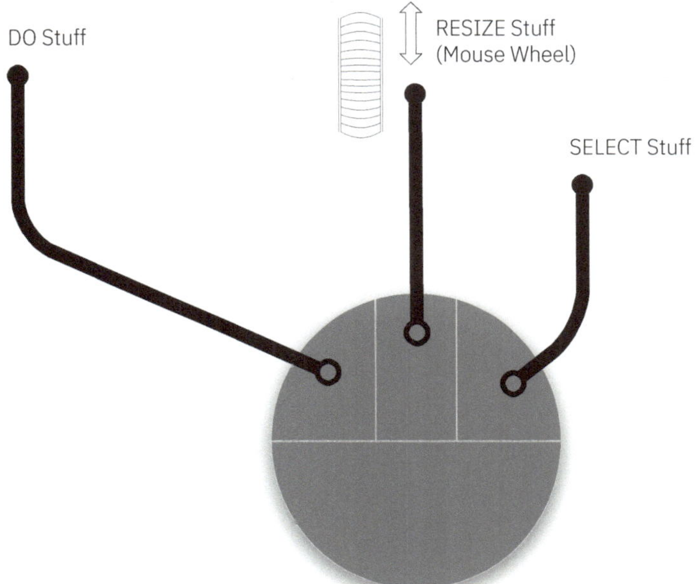

SELECT   **Right-mouse-button**: Tap to select or deselect existing shapes (use **-Del** to remove). Once a polygon or other shape is selected the wheel should adjust the lineweight. Press and drag on a previously unselected shape to move it around or, alternatively, press and use the wheel to resize selected shapes. Further menu options appear to the lower left when items are selected.

To deselect all simply double-tap on the canvas background.

Your Mouse

Mouse and cursor

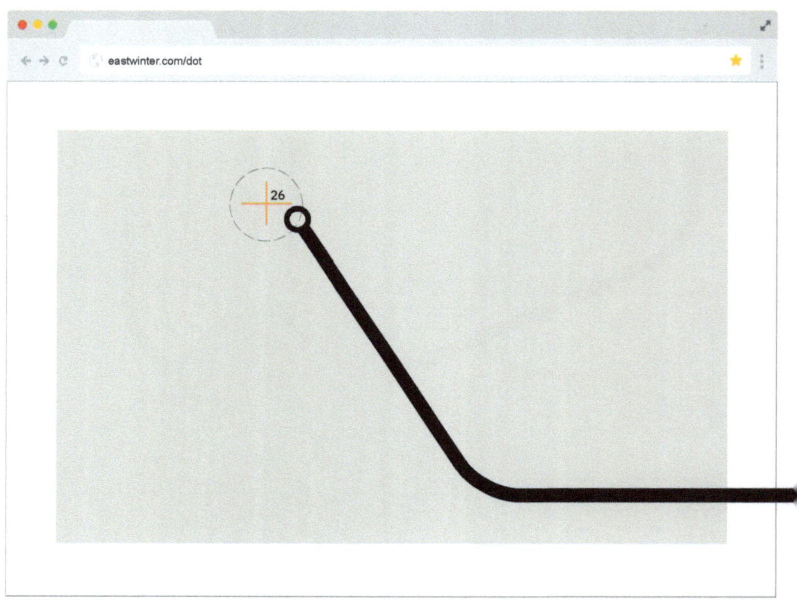

Dot's basic layout: When the mouse is over the canvas area

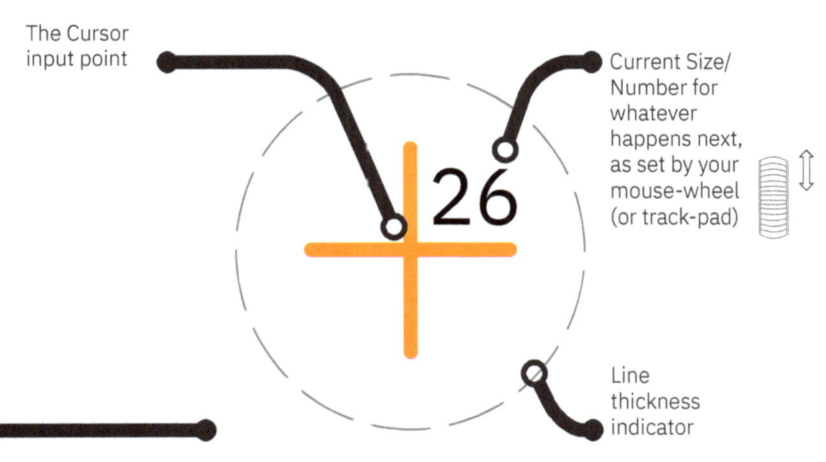

Dot's basic drawing implement (Cursor / Brush / Tool)

Drawing: DotsLinesOther

In playing with the toolset [8] you may see that some tools invite additional options to the lower left, for example; '**brsh**' [7] introduces a small slider which can be clicked on or wheeled over to set the amount of ink in the brush—the higher the ink level the longer the brush stroke line lasts before fading out.

'**dots**' introduces '**zero**' and '**togN**', the former restarts the dot numbering sequence, the latter sets whether or not to use numbers. After one or two dots are made two further submenu options of '**rNum**' and '**join**', the former works only where numbered dots have been deleted and a recount is required, and the latter simply joins dots with a new polygon—to be deleted, resized, colour changed or moved. And '**shuf**' shuffles numbers.

'**poly**' works with single taps, one to start, one for each corner point, and a swift double-tap in the same position to complete the shape.

'**rand**' generates a random polygon. The current cursor number defines the number of corners given to the new polygon. Selecting rectangles beforehand will determine where newly generated polygons are composed.

7. **brsh thickness can be varied mid-stroke by using the mouse wheel simultaneously—whilst moving and pressing the left mouse button.**

    If using a laptop with mouse, or with pen and tablet, you may find 'scrolling' on the trackpad (in place of mouse wheel action) to be more effective.

8. **Left-mouse-double-click on pen_ to invoke Magenta-sketch-RNN. A machine learning Tensorflow based sketch toy—that sketches back.**

    This is the second of two imported external code demonstrations. The implementation here is sketchy at best but may improve overtime.

rect

pen_ [8]

brsh

dots

poly

rand

pen_: MagentaSketchRNN

Activating the **pen_** tool, and selecting **auto** (the lower left sub-menu)will call up Magenta-sketch [9] RNN [10] and place the **pen_** in a new dynamic state of play. It may take a few seconds for the machine-learning models to load behind the scenes, after which a notification to the bottom left will inform you. Working in a 'call and response' process subsequent shapes drawn on the canvas area will invoke a drawing response from Magenta-sketch in the manner of the selected machine-learning model.

To change the model, simply click on the **mods** (visible only when **auto** is active) menu item and a list of objects will appear. Magenta-sketch is a machine learning system which has been trained on hundreds of thousands of hand-drawn sketches—a form of communal 'experience' of each object. However, response drawings made by Magenta are unique replies [11] informed by the characteristics of your (call) drawings. Magenta's **pen_** like responses are temporary. To retain all of a set simply tap the 'a' key (select all) or select individual lines using the right mouse button. Once selected they are automatically retained, and can by resized/coloured. Select any other tool to return to normality.

9. **Written by David Ha and Douglas Eck, as part of the TensorFlow.js Magenta team.**

   For details on implementing this in your own code please see their Github page:

   https://github.com/magenta/magenta-demos/tree/master/sketch-rnn-js

10. **RNN = Recurrent Neural Network. A form of machine learning configuration.**

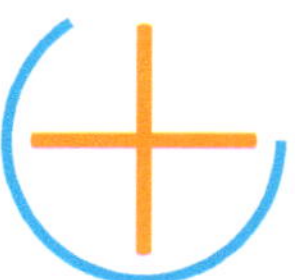

11. **Using the mousewheel in this mode invokes an arc shape, framing the cursor. The greater the sweep of the arc, the more relaxed (in theory) the response in relation to the model.**

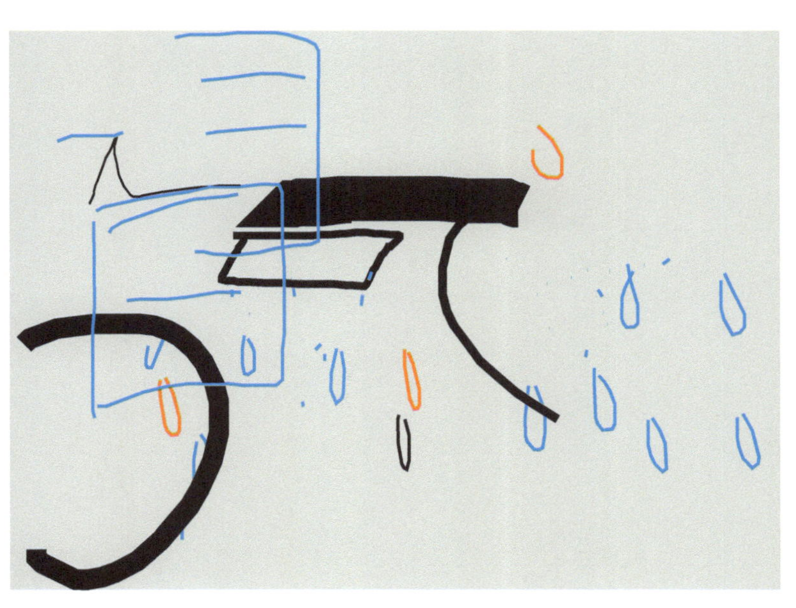

Call and response. luxanbolts

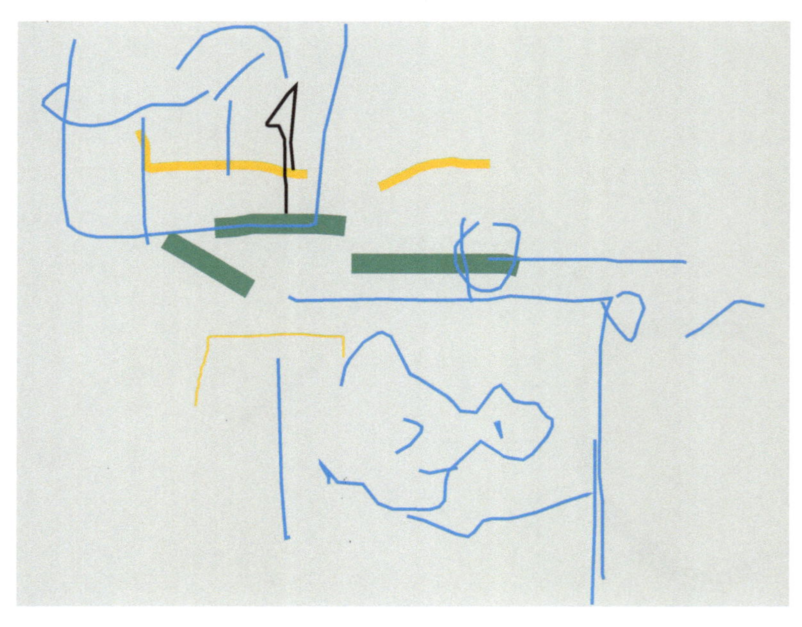

The game called real-life. luxandbolts

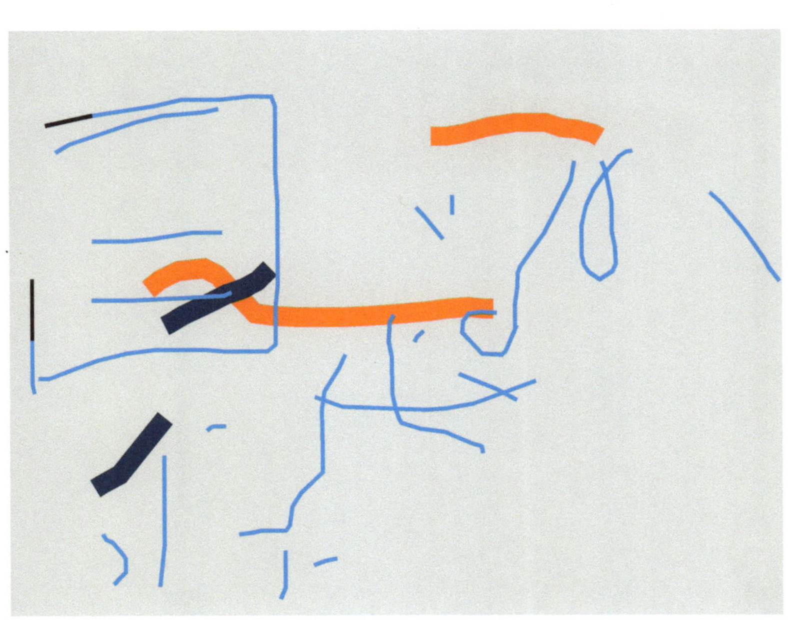

Lightness of being. luxandbolts

brsh

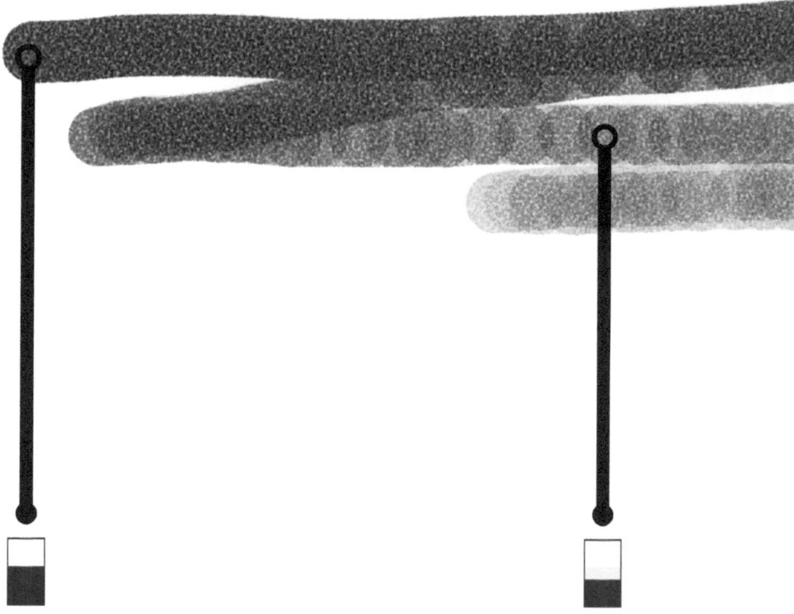

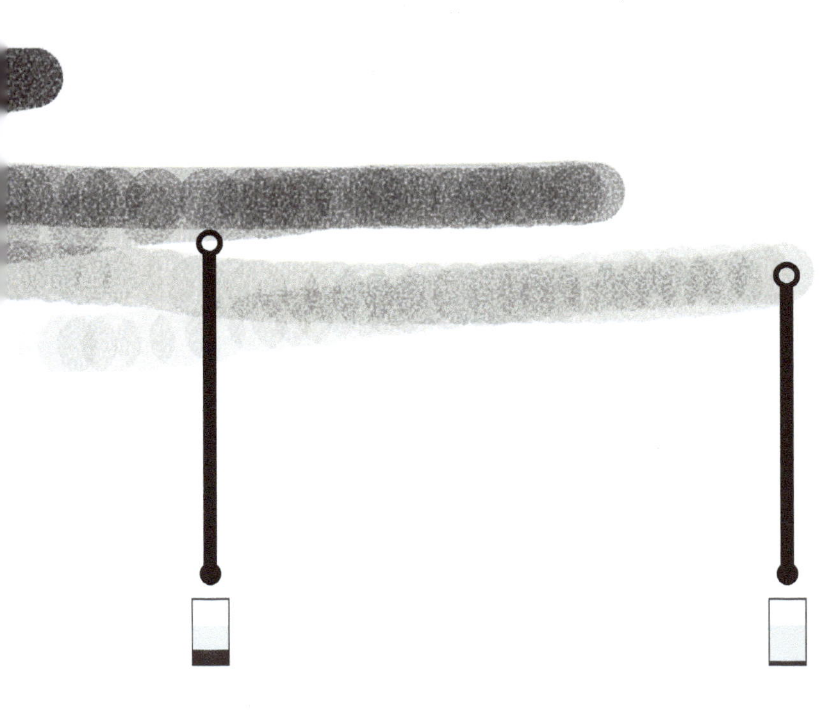

*Ink depletion of the '**brsh**' tool*

Selecting

To **select**:   tap on an element with the right-mouse-button, or tap again to deselect, to deselect everything use a single tap on the esc key. Selected elements take on a temporarily animated red hue. [12] [13]
To **rotate**:   tap to select, press the command key, whilst using the wheel.
To **move**:   *press[R]—drag—release* on a previously unselected element.
To **resize**:   *press[R]—wheel—release* on a previously unselected element.
To **adjust lineweight**: tap to select, then wheel (not for all elements).

Submenu [lower left corner]:

'-Del'   appears as an option to remove selected elements.
'updn'   moves a selection to the front (up) or the back (dn).
'dupl'   appears where elements are selected—this option creates a
           duplicate on top, which can then be repositioned.
'frag'   appears where a polygon is selected—with this option a new
           sequence of dots is created at the polygons corner points. Useful
           for planning and creating new dot drawings with more control.
'mask'   appears where one polygon and one image are selected—where
           the polygon should be over the image.

12. Double tap with the right mouse button in an area with no objects to de-select anything currently highlighted.

13. Selected items can also be cut, copied, or pasted between open drawing windows using the standard key commands listed later.

nb. There is no UNDO function, and there are *no* plans to introduce one.

Selection:

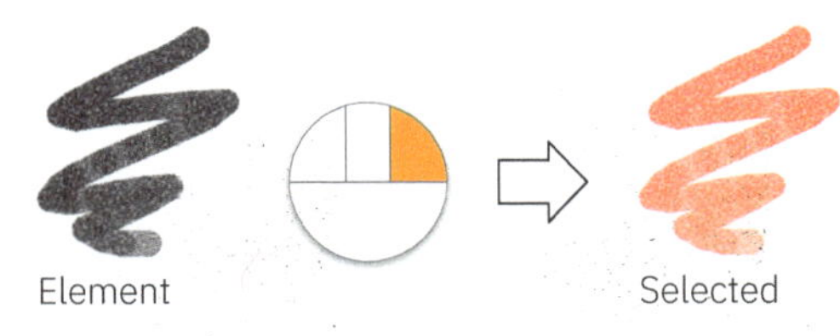

Rotation:

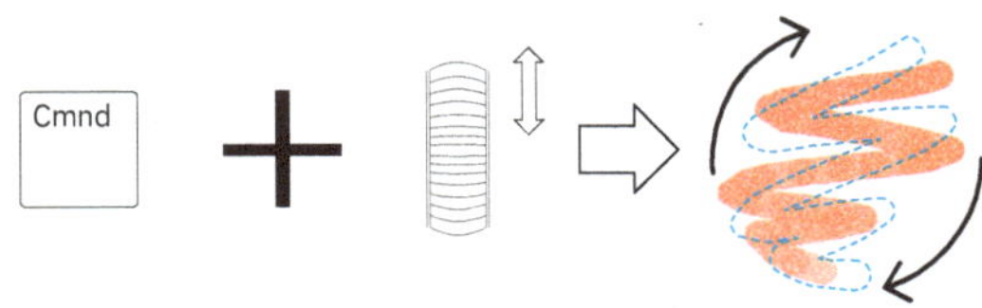

Movement:

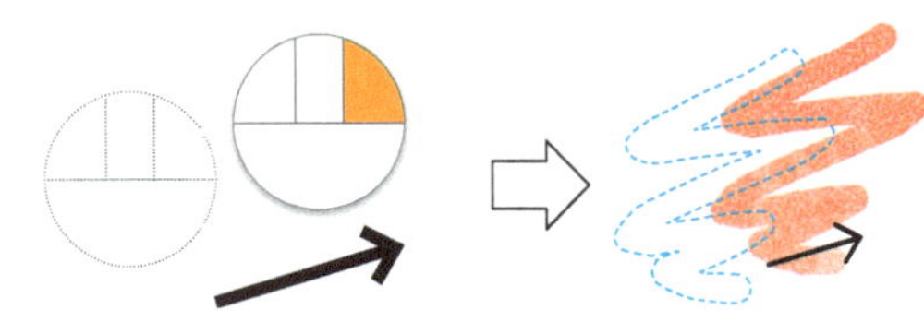

Scaling:

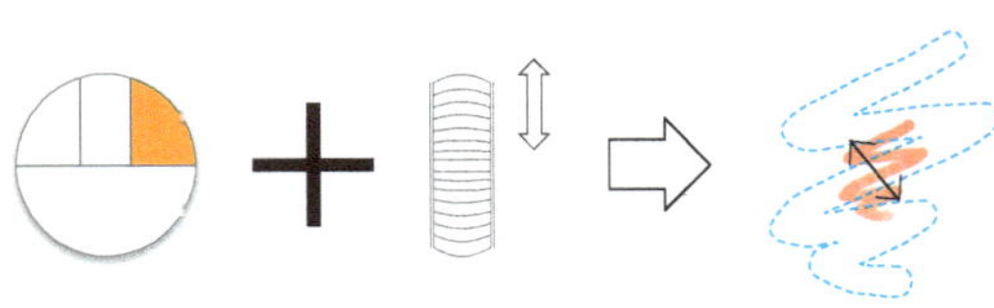

Lineweight:

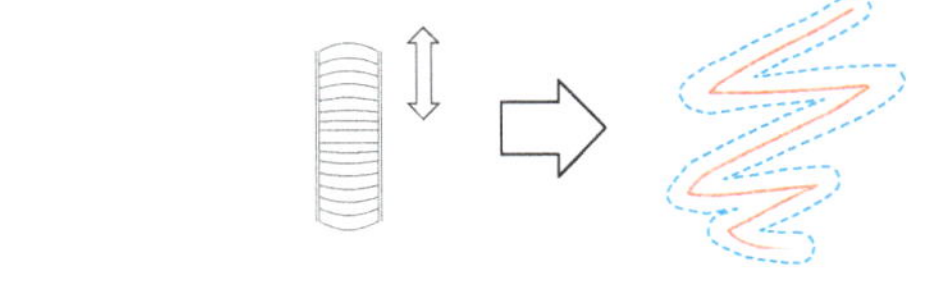

Dot's selection techniques

colr

Dot starts drawing with a default dark grey tone. By using the colour palette a wider spectrum of options becomes available, and it is worth remembering the keyboard shortcut; the Shift key for momentary speedy access, or the Caps-lock key for those moments you need to work on the palette itself. At first a default palette is presented of generally complementary colours, alongside to the left we have submenu options.

From the top, 'line' changes to 'fill' when tapped, when 'line' is visible colours selected with the left mouse button change subsequent outline colours for newly drawn elements—whilst changing any currently selected elements. When 'fill' is visible the body colour of elements will be adjusted.

Below you'll find 'cstm'; this introduces the custom palette. The first items here are preset brush types indicated typically by a number and letter only and more brush types may be added in time. The very first item removes special brush types. Beyond these the remaining space is set to await newly mixed colours.

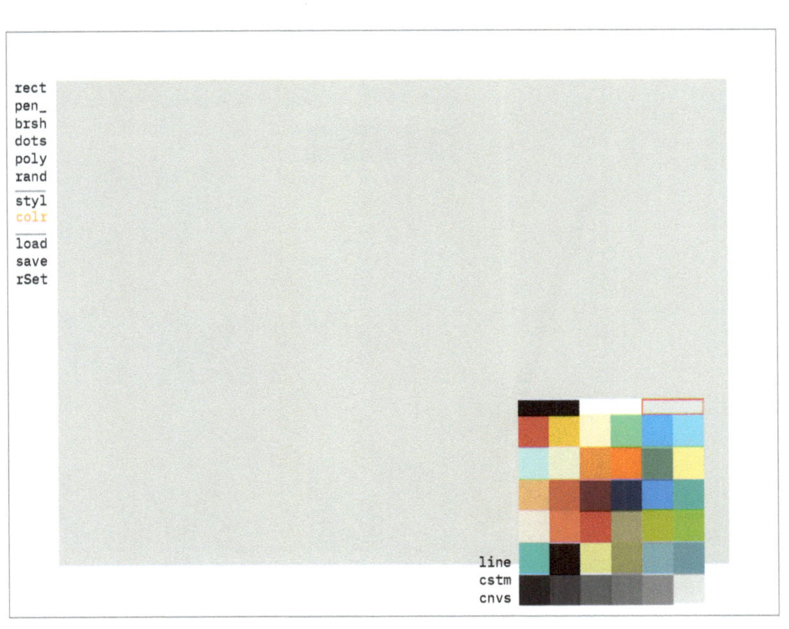

The Colour palette in context [Caps Lock / Shift keys]

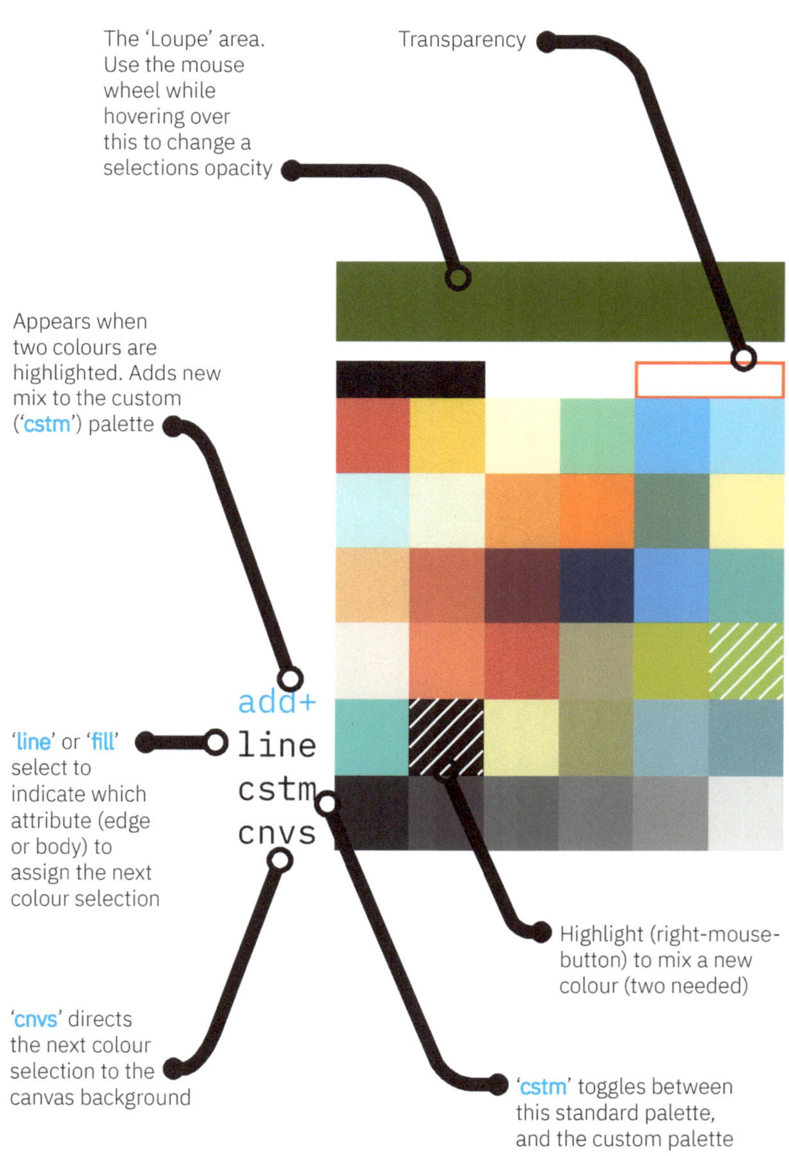

The Colour palette

The last submenu item is '**cnvs**' and, when selected, primes the canvas background colour itself to receive the next selected colour

Within the default colour palette taps from the left mouse button will select colours for immediate use of the next drawing tool. However, taps with the right mouse button will highlight or deselect colours to mix to create new colours, which in turn will appear in the custom palette area.

To create a new custom colour, simply highlight two colours using the right mouse button. In doing so a new menu option called '**add+**' will appear in blue, and this will attempt to create a new blended mix in the custom area. The custom palette is not interested in duplicates of new colours. Alternatively, to remove a custom colour, select the custom colour with the right mouse button and a '**del-**' item will appear, allowing the removal of the selected colour.

Custom colours are saved automagically within drawing files.

Loading and Saving

Please save your drawings! Think of this website as a drawing space and a functioning app. Using the 'save' menu option will download a '**sketch.dots**' file which can be renamed accordingly elsewhere on the computer's file manager on condition the file extension remains unchanged. This file is in principle only compatible with dot.

Images can be saved separately by selecting them (right mouse button) before tapping 'save' with the **left mouse button**.

Drawings can be exported as SVG [14] files by tapping 'save' with the **right mouse button**.

Loading is equally straightforward: images [15] or previously saved drawings may be dragged into the canvas area (one at a time) for continued editing—or of course by using the 'load' menu option.

Just as for any other app the keyboard shortcuts are **ctrl+s** to save, and **ctrl+o** to open a file via your browser file dialogue.

---

14. **SVG = Scalable Vector Graphic.**
   A native Adobe® file format compatible with many online and desktop illustration applications. Within the context of Dot SVG files have fewer editing options than native 'sketch.dots' files if reloaded.

15. **Images may also be pasted into dot from other websites:**
   after right clicking on an image of another webpage and choosing 'Copy Image Address' of the pop-up menu. This avoids the trouble of saving images [does not yet support .webp]

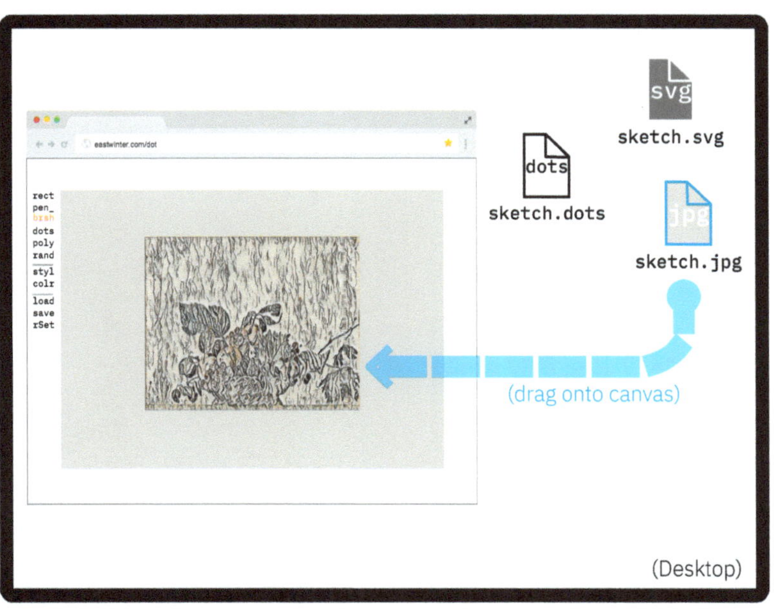

Loading files

46

MagentaImage: StyleTransfer

In the spirit of abstraction, of experimentation, and of play, a version of 'Magenta Image' a Machine Learning Style Transfer function is woven into the code. This is 'An open source research project exploring the role of machine learning as a tool in the creative process' built by Reiichiro Nakano, Vincent Dumoulin and David Ha on the TensorFlow Machine Learning framework.

This toy lives under the 'styl' menu tool. As for many new toys/tools this implementation has its own particular way of working, its own procedure. To avoid over hype: it requires some patience, and some experimentation, and even after, the results might not inspire you.

As an aim, with this tool, the computer is asked to produce a NEW image using a ***given*** image, taking inspiration from a ***style*** image. This means the tool wants to see TWO images, a GIVEN image, and a STYLE (transfer) image. The sequence is: (1) Set STYLE transfer image, (2) define the GIVEN image, (3) generate a NEW image. If you have drawings, be sure to save them before/during this process!

1. The STYLE image is essential.y any image in the new grey mini canvas that pops up when the **styl** menu option is active. Tapping on this 'brings in' an image or a drawing. To move an uploaded image into this area, one image should be selected before then tapping on the style area mini canvas. To use a drawing instead as a style image then there should be a drawing with no images present in the main canvas before tapping on the style mini canvas.

2. Now that a STYLE transfer image is set, we address the GIVEN image:

   a. Double tap the 'esc' keyboard button, or double tap on '**rSet**' on the menu to clear the canvas.
   b. Bring in a new image and SELECT it (right mouse button), OR sketch a new drawing.
   c. This is now the GIVEN image.

3. Tap once on the mini canvas presently holding the STYLE transfer image, then wait patiently while Magenta contemplates. Thinking time will vary depending on the size and complexity of the drawing, and the hardware computing power hosting the browser. The result should eventually appear at the centre of the canvas but positioned in the background [to move forward please select it and use the '**frnt**' submenu option or the 'up' cursor arrow on the keyboard.

Perhaps experiment using a drawing to create a new image in the style of another drawing, or in the style of an image, or a new image in the style of a drawing given an image, or maybe a new image in the style of an image given an image. Recycle, rinse, repeat, and somewhere in this method—in a moment—you might find your process.

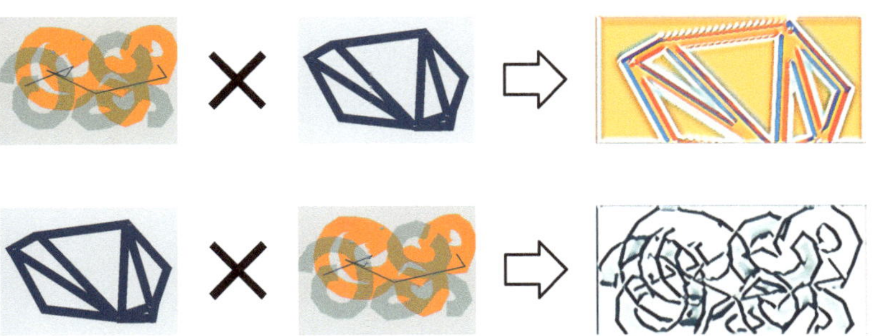

GIVEN image ...in the style of STYLE image ...leading to ...RESULT images.

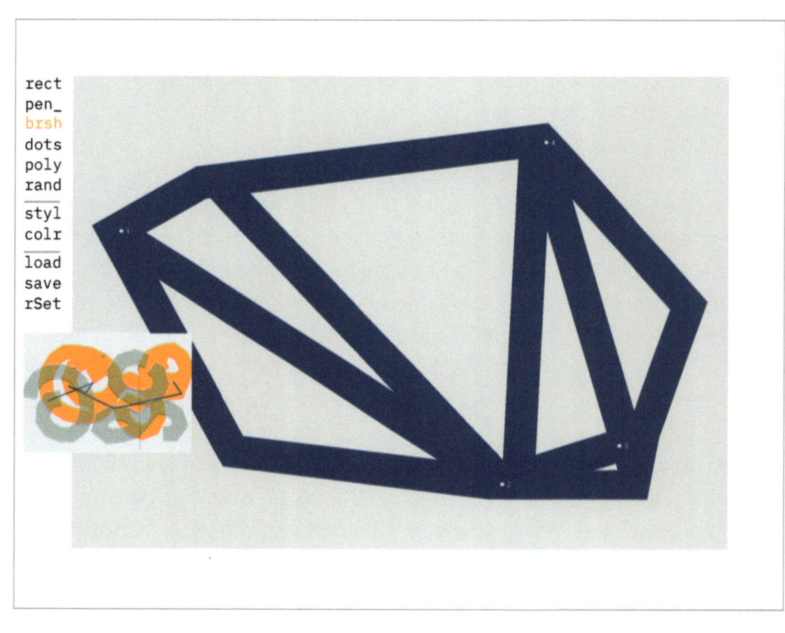

STYLE drawind and GIVEN source drawing in position

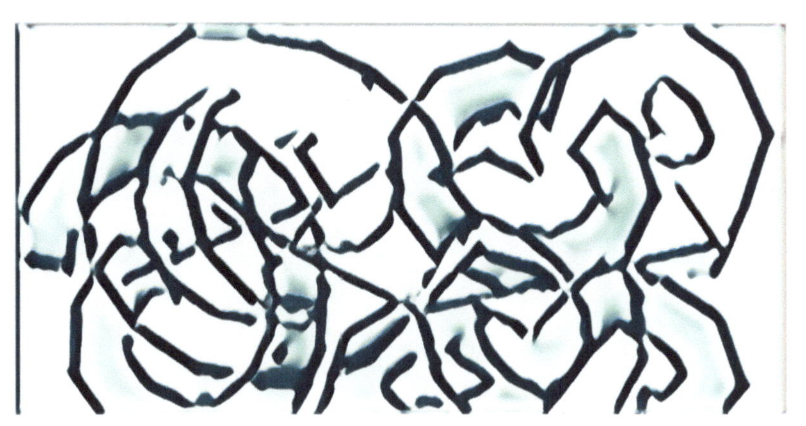

RESULT Image

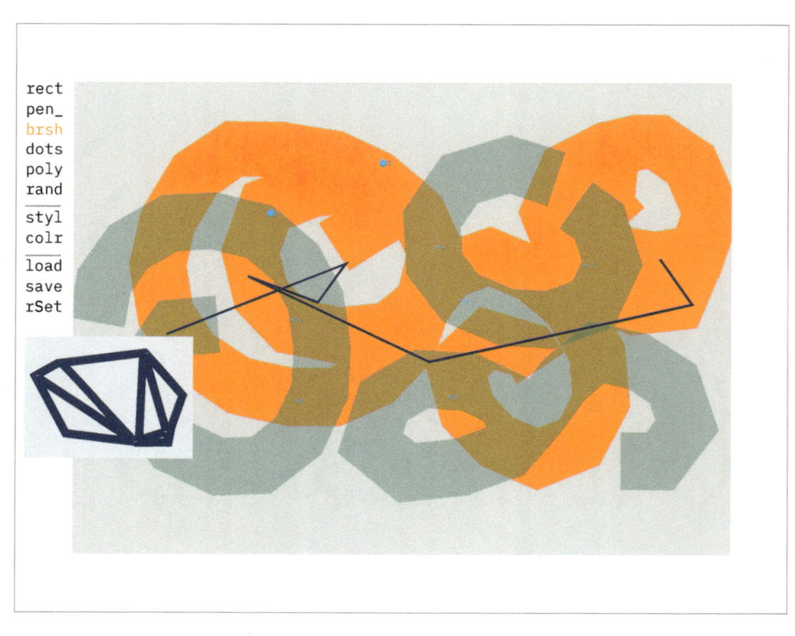

STYLE drawind and GIVEN source drawing in position

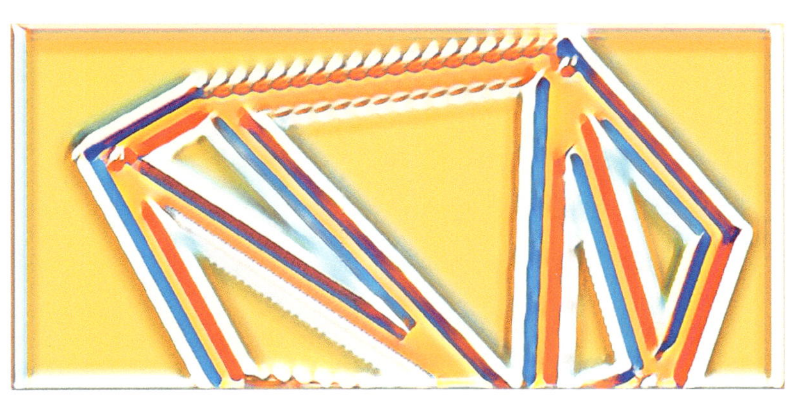

RESULT Image

Keyboard manoeuvres:

Drawing Tools:

2   —freehand inked line

4   —draw a rectangle

5   —freehand drawing

6   —dots or circles

8   —draw polygons

0   —restart dot numbering from 1

r   —create randomised polygon,
        use the wheel to set the
        number of corners beforehand

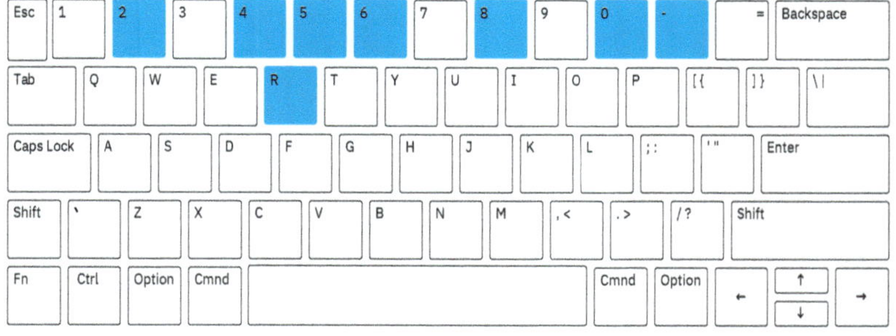

Selection actions:

backspace   —**delete** selection and clear the styl minicanvas

up / **down** arrows   —**bring to front** or **send to back**

-   —**remove** images

d   —**duplicate** selected

=   —add numbers to a selected polygon

m   —**mask** [after only one image and one poly selected]

cmmd + option   —**marquee** selection [may screw with positioning!]

esc   —tap once to deselect or double tap to clear all elements from a canvas [but not the styl area]

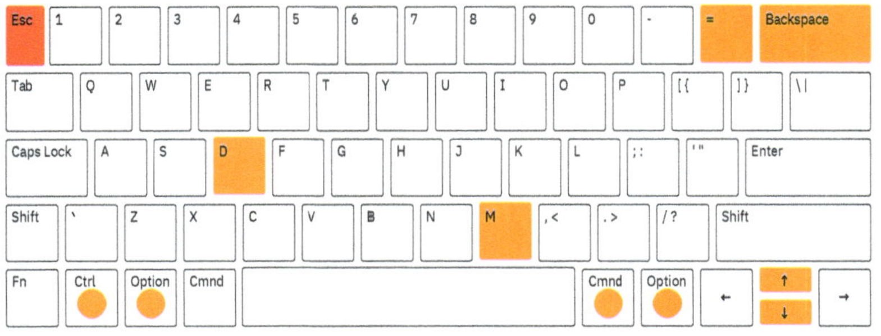

Extended actions:

/   —renumber dots (after individual dots have been removed)

s   —shuffle dots

.   —toggles whether or not the following dots will be numbered

Enter   —connect existing numbered dots

Tab   —toggle style transfer area

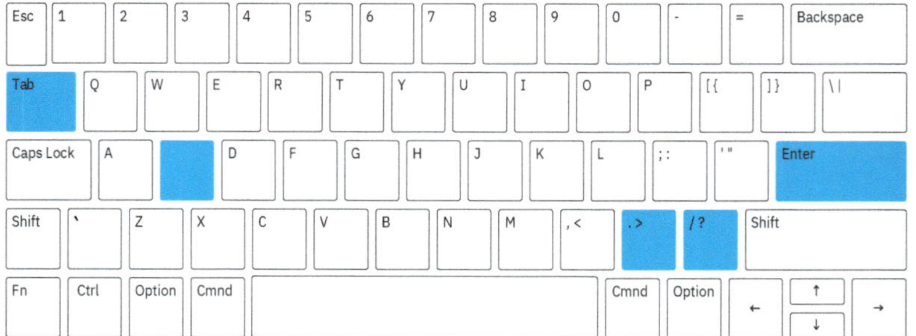

Colours:

caps lock / **shift key**   —colour palette

;   —selects the canvas itself to change the
                                        background colour

Left-mouse tap on colour   —select new colour

Right-mouse tap on colour   —select two colours to mix
Use the **right-mouse-button** to tap on two different colours, tap on the
newly appeared 'add+' to create a new custom blend

Mouse wheel over loupe to adjust opacity of selected shapes

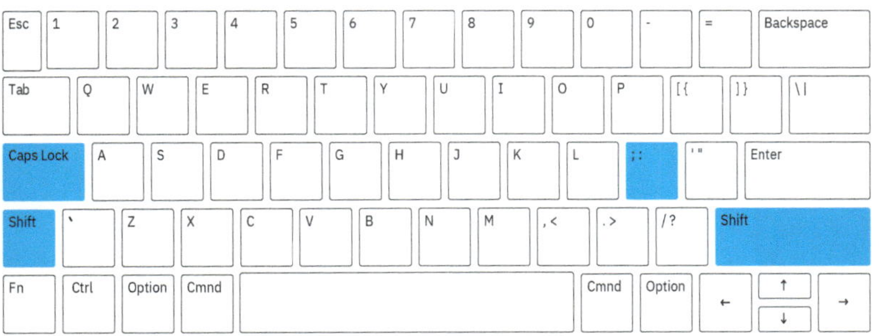

Utility actions:

ctrl + s   —**save** drawing   (Cmnd + s on Apple Mac)

ctrl + o   —**open** drawing/image   (Cmnd + o on Apple Mac)

ctrl + p   —**print** then save as pdf (Cmnd + p on Apple Mac)

ctrl + a   —**select all** in drawing (Cmnd + a on Apple Mac)

ctrl + x, c, v   —**cut, copy, paste** content (Cmnd + x,c,v Apple Mac)

`   —toggle **dark mode**

space   —toggle **menu visibility**

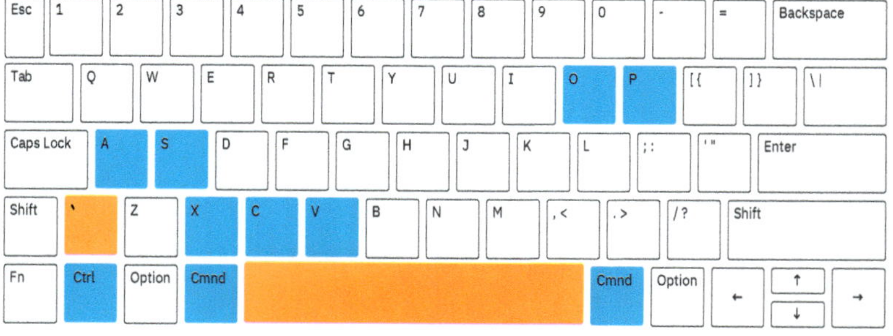

STYL transfer cheat sheet:

machine learning 'style transfer' (experimental) summary instructions:

i.   [you will make and lose two drawings in exchange for a (weird) stylised interpretation]

ii.   create a busy drawing to become the 'style reference'

iii.   click on the 'styl' menu option

iv.   click on the new grey box that appears

v.   press the 'esc' key or 'rset' menu option

vi.   create a new different drawing

vii.   click on the style drawing

viii.   wait, while your computer contemplates

ix.   ...behold new image!

x.   do other stuff on top of it.

Tooling

Between the artist and the drawing tool there is often a kind of dynamic, a relationship of sorts, and here within this dynamic there may be a moment for a conversation. Between the mark an artist intends to put into play, and the way a tool goes about implementing it in play. An artist might at some point have in mind to draw a diagonal green line, for example, but the brush tool in use only holds so much ink, and so the line fades as it extends as the ink runs out, and so the artist moves to respond by using lighter repeated strokes at intervals. The line no longer appears to fade but the many starting points with denser ink levels are now more apparent, and the line has a different quality, which the artist in turn may choose to accept—if the line absolutely had to be consistent then a different tool would have been called for. Perhaps this dialogue (between thought and outcome) factors in the artist's experience, familiarity with this particular tool, and certainty in the artist's intention, all in conversation with the tool's physical capabilities (its presence-at-hand), its relationship to other materials (inks, papers, screens…) and their respective attributes, and its inherent processes— the way it wants to work.

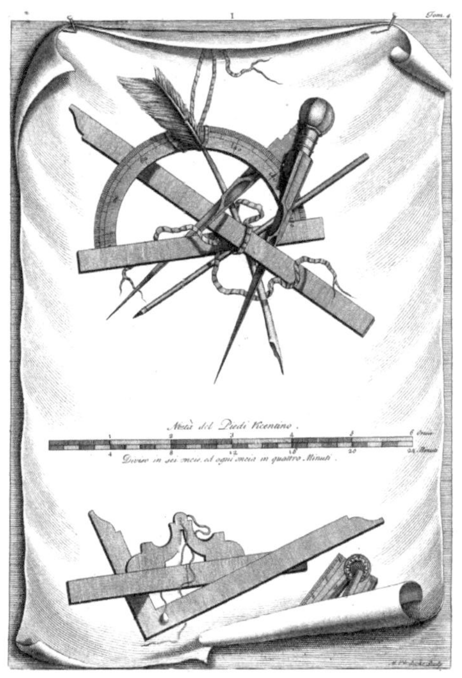

Above. **Michael van der Gucht (1660–1725), Frontispiece to Vol. 4 of the third edition in English of Palladio's Four Books of Architecture, c. 1724.**
Engraving on watermarked laid paper, 453 × 284 mm. found via Drawing Matter Archives: www.drawingmatter.org

This first point; the artist's familiarity with the tool at hand, and the last point; the tool's inherent processes frame the conversation such that; where an artist is completely familiar with a tool (including its processes) it disappears as a tool, becoming part of a hand, then part of a thought, leaving just the intention, and the line—here maybe now there is no longer a need or space for dialogue—as the tool is rendered transparent. In the other situation, where an artist is unfamiliar with a new tool at-hand then here we're likely to find a more awkward discussion; between what is aimed for and what is achievable, and whether a (usually slightly unexpected) outcome is actually more interesting, or completely unacceptable, or maybe just okay—a compromise. This dynamic sequence of decisions, actions, and reflection might be better described as a state of play, in the sense of a creativity at play. Yet; *'if all you have is a hammer, everything starts to look like a nail'* [16] and so, how much is the tool and its preferred processes, in this particular moment, augmenting the line or influencing a possibility?

These thoughts might be experienced on paper when learning to sketch. The internal difficulty sometimes seen when switching to pen and ink—after having just begun to familiarise with pencil—and the subtle shift in approach somehow changes things, even though both tools make lines.

In the digital arena, these properties are constructed, and defined, in part by software developers—as a community of Blacksmiths (of which, for this amateur, each line of dot's code was hard won) over a longer conversation with a user community of creatives and in part a legacy of familiarity with previous tools. So to return, this discussion should perhaps first be had between the artist; and the application. Around the intended work, the negotiations, compromise, and harmonics. Between the creative practitioner and the digital environment as drawing tool.

Asking these questions and engaging in the dynamic of drawing itself, may provide a more fruitful answer than anything that could be said in words. As such, we encourage you to play, to work-around the quirks of this web-app, to 'take a line for a walk' [17], and see what happens?

16. Maslow, A.H, 1966. *The psychology of science a reconnaissance.*

17. Klee, P. and Moholy-Nagy, S., 1953. Pedagogical sketchbook. London: Faber & Faber.

"An active line on a walk, moving freely, without goal. A walk for a walk's sake. The mobility agent, is a point, shifting its position forward." [lesson #1]

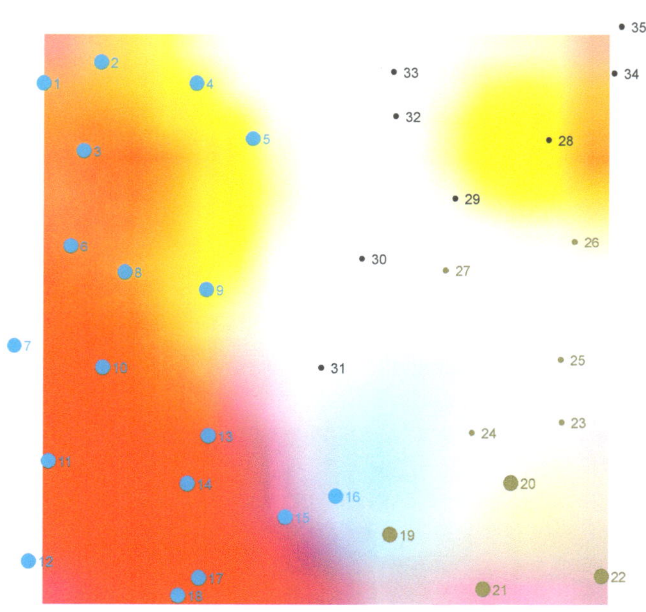

No one thing. luxandbolts.

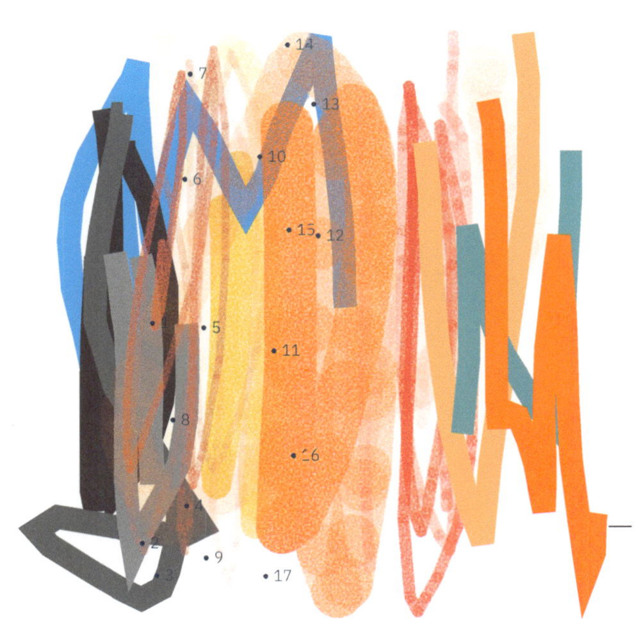

There from then. luxandbolts.

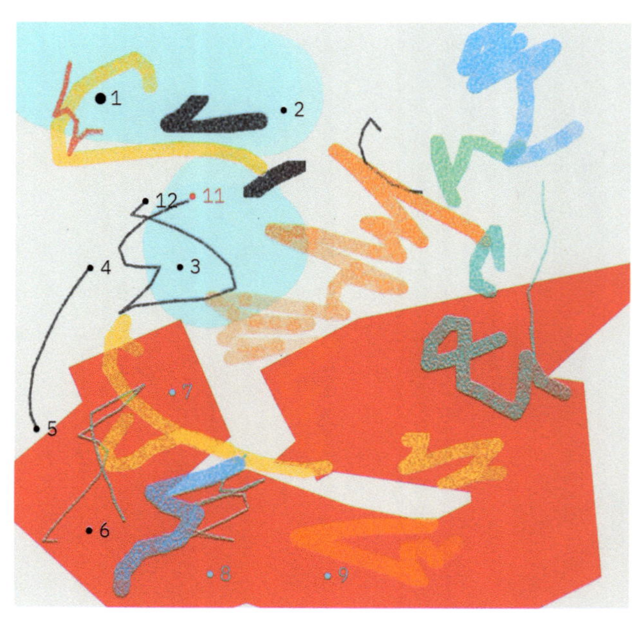

At play. luxandbolts.

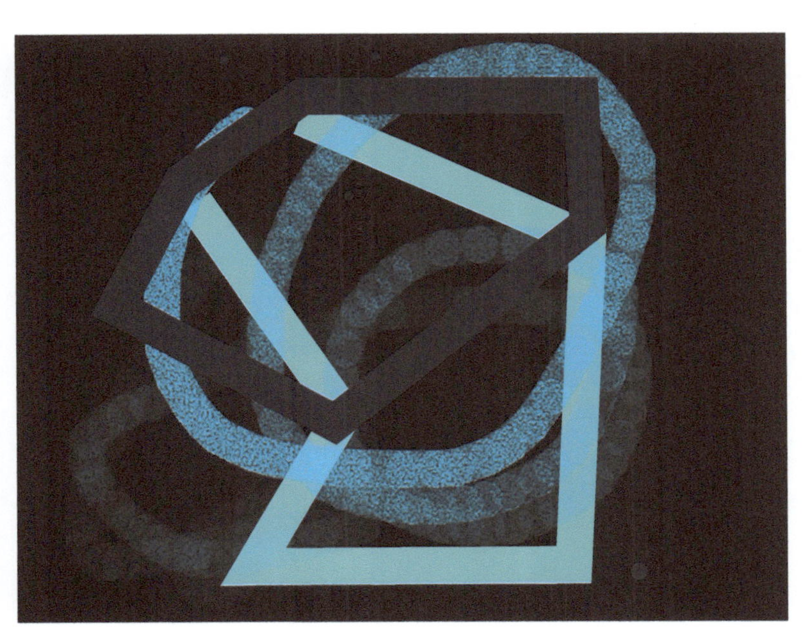

An invitation. luxandbolts.

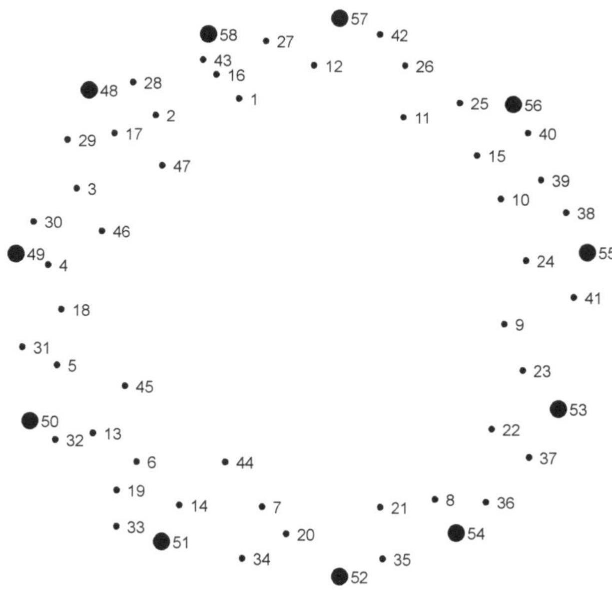

57
58
27
42
43
12
16
26
1
48
28
25
56
2
11
40
17
29
15
47
39
3
10
38
30
46
24
55
49
4
41
18
9
31
5
23
45
53
50
22
32
13
37
6
44
19
8
36
14
7
21
33
20
54
51
34
35
52

The rest. luxandbolts.

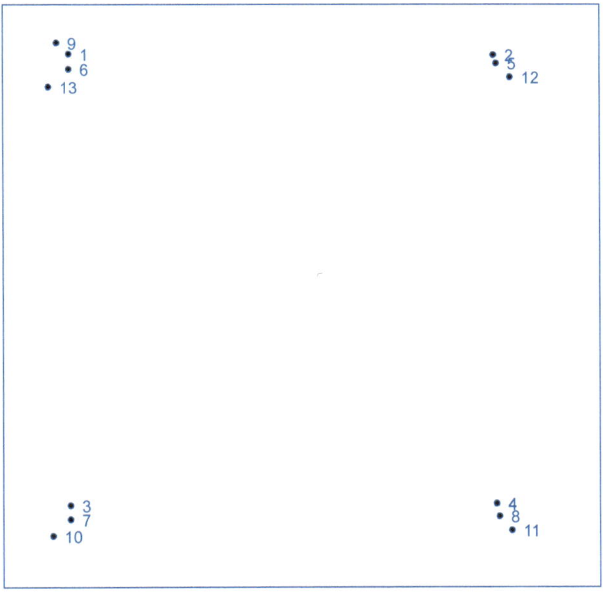

68

Limits of Control. luxandbolts.

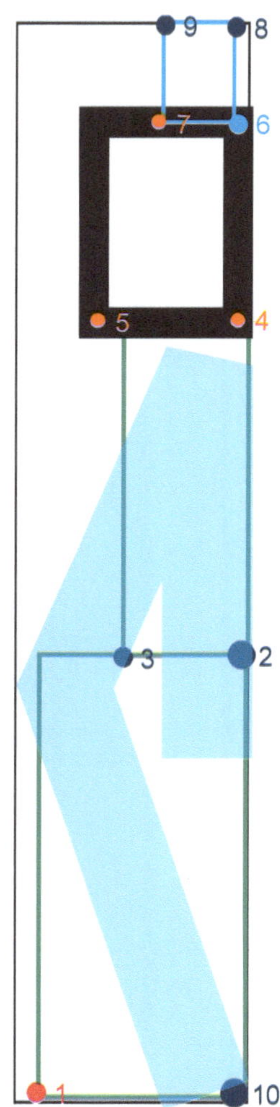

Schema a, part I. luxandbolts.

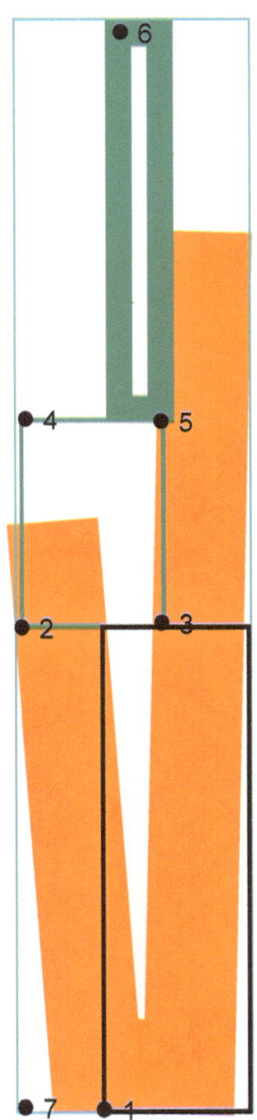

Schema α, part II. luxandbolts.

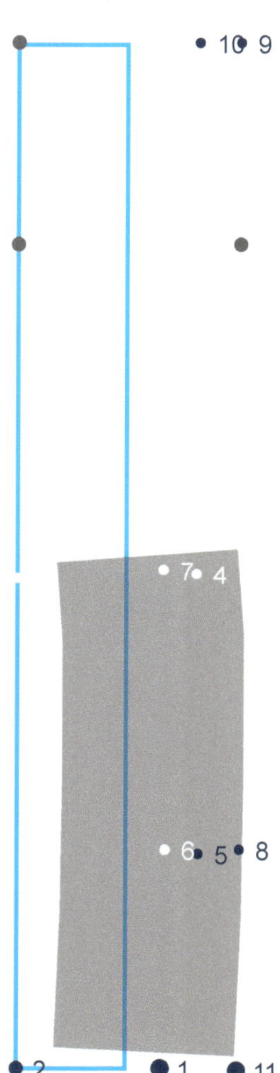

Garden of lost numbers, west. luxandbolts.

71

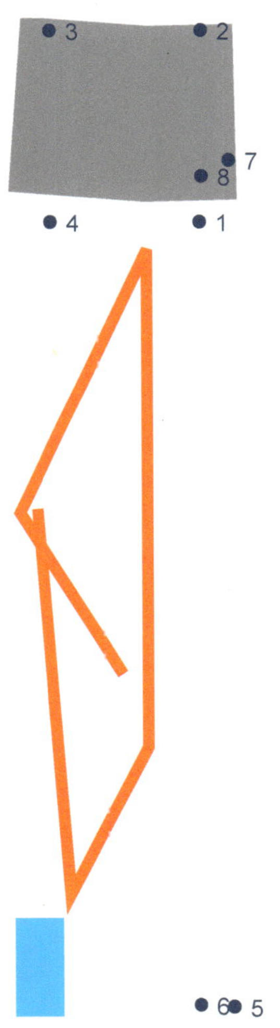

Garden of lost numbers, north. luxandbolts.

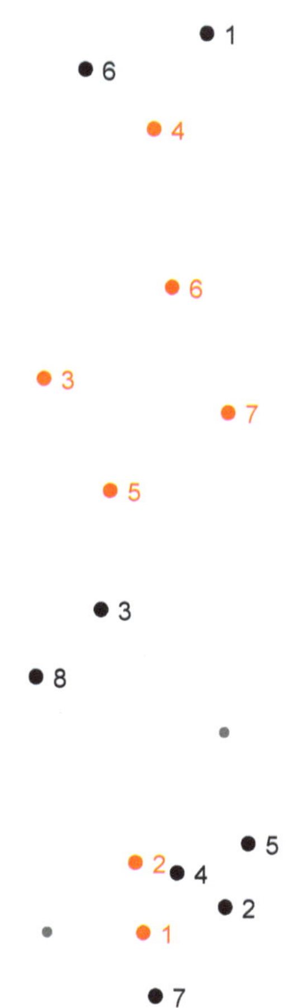

Network theory, part I. luxandbolts.

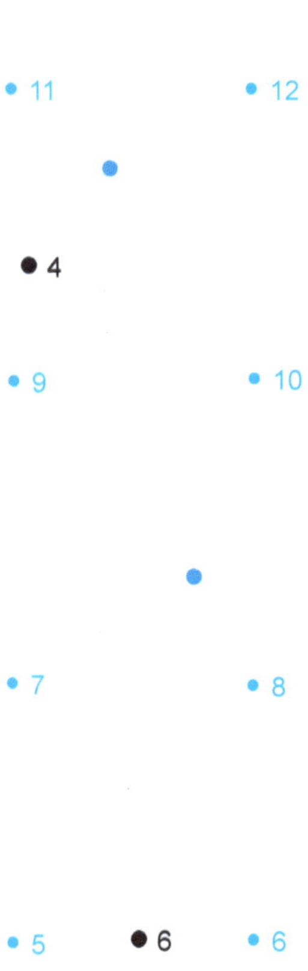
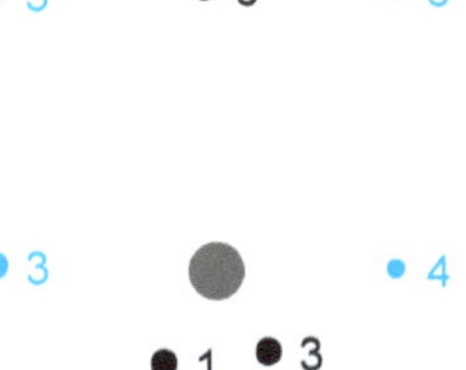

Network theory, part II. luxandbolts.

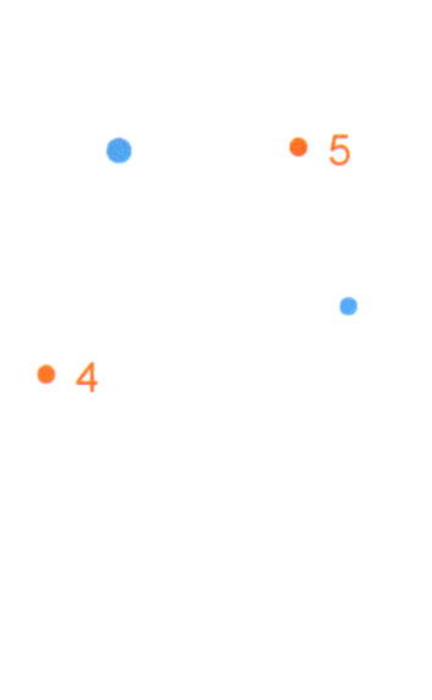
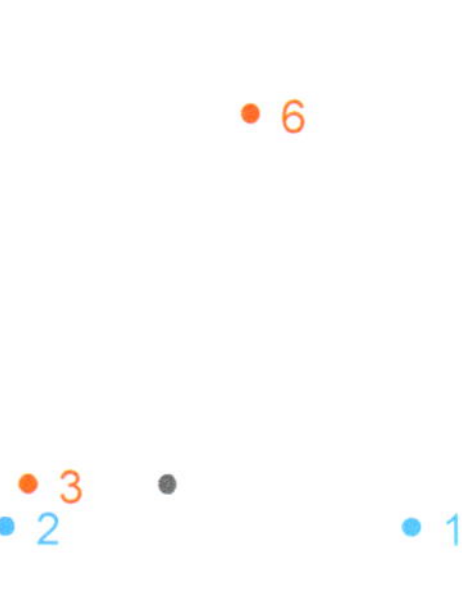

Network theory, part III. luxandbolts.

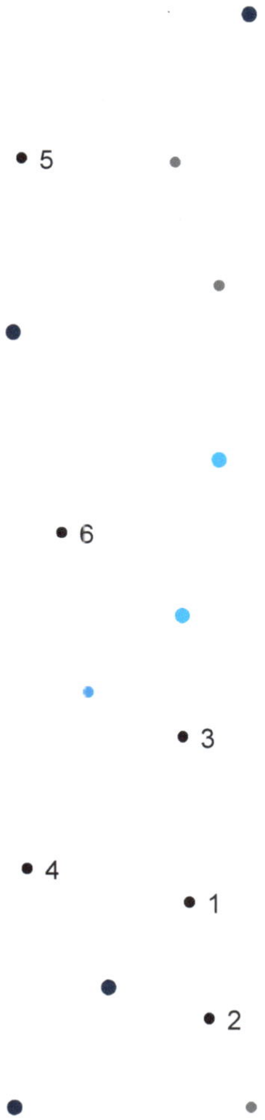

Network theory, part IV. luxandbolts.

Acknowledgements

Luxandbolts wishes to express a heartfelt thanks to the various artists who took time out of their schedules to humour me in this generally non-essential exercise. In particular: A.K (Tokyo), Y.M (Tokyo), R.A (Toronto), R.W, J.L (San Francisco), E.S (Athens), Dr E.L, V.L (Shanghai), I.H, S.B, A.B & S.B (Brighton), S.V, M.vd.W, S.N.M, M.W.C & P.W, research supervisors C.F and N.K, and E.L for her editorial assist. Plus, the team at East Winter® Books for hosting the app and indulging this project.

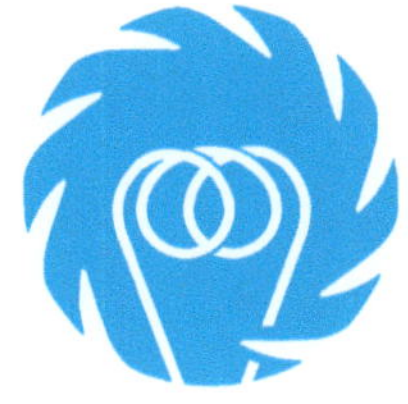

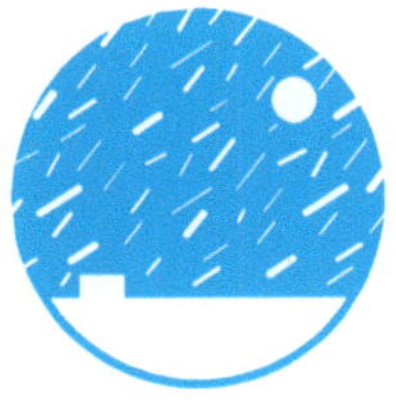

Lightning Source UK Ltd.
Milton Keynes UK
UKHW051320150920
369918UK00009B/113

9 780993 504648